Autumn
Publishing

Published in 2017
by Autumn Publishing
Cottage Farm
Sywell
NN6 0BJ
www.igloobooks.com

LEO002 0517
2 4 6 8 10 9 7 5 3 1
ISBN 978-1-78810-663-4

The publisher would like to thank Alamy for permission to use the following image:
page 28 (top and background), Steve Allen Travel Photography / Alamy Stock Photo.
All other images provided by iStockphoto.com.

Cover designed by Richard Sykes
Interiors designed by Starry Dog Books

Printed and manufactured in China

OVER
100
FACTS FOR KIDS
FLAGS OF THE WORLD

Autumn
Publishing

The World

FACT 1 There are about 195 countries in the world today. Not everybody agrees on the number.

FACT 2 A country is an area of land ruled by one government.

FACT 3 The land in the world is split into seven blocks called continents.

Atlantic Ocean

FACT 4 Antarctica is the only continent that is not split up into countries.

FACT 5 Africa has about 55 countries, more than any other continent.

6

Continents

- North America
- South America
- Africa
- Europe
- Asia
- Oceania
- Antarctica

FACT 6 Only 29 per cent of the world's surface is land. The rest is water.

FACT 7 The Pacific Ocean is bigger than all the world's land put together.

Pacific Ocean

FACT 8 Asia is the biggest continent.

FACT 9 About 4.5 billion people live in Asia. That's more than the rest of the world put together.

FACT 10 Oceania is the smallest continent.

North and Central America

FACT 11 The United States of America is one country made up of 50 smaller areas called states.

FACT 12 There are 50 stars on the US flag, one for each of the 50 states.

FACT 13 The US flag got its 50th star in 1960, when Hawaii was added as a state.

FACT 14 The leaf on Canada's flag comes from the country's national tree, the maple.

FACT 15 The eagle and cactus on Mexico's flag are symbols of the Aztec people that ruled Mexico 500 years ago.

FACT 16 Dominica is one of only two countries to have purple on its flag. The other is Nicaragua.

FACT 17 The flag of Haiti features weapons ready to defend the country's freedom.

FACT 18 Dominica and Haiti are in the Caribbean, a group of islands in the Atlantic Ocean.

South America

FACT 19 The constellations on Brazil's flag show the sky on the night Brazil became a country.

FACT 20 The words across the middle of Brazil's flag are the country's motto, which means "Order and Progress".

FACT 21 Much of Brazil is covered by the Amazon rainforest, the biggest jungle in the world.

Amazon rainforest

FACT 22 The bird on the flag of Bolivia is an Andean condor. Its wings stretch 3 m (10 ft).

FACT 23 The red stripe on Bolivia's flag stands for the blood of its soldiers.

FACT 24 The mountain on the flag of Ecuador is Chimborazo, the country's highest peak. It is 6,263 m (20,549 ft) high.

FACT 25 The boat on Ecuador's flag is a real trading vessel called the *Guayas*.

FACT 26 The first copy of the Chilean flag was stolen by protesters in 1980. They gave it back more than 20 years later.

FACT 27 The sun on the flag of Argentina is a copy of the country's first coin.

The United Kingdom

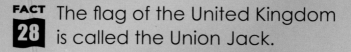

FACT 28 The flag of the United Kingdom is called the Union Jack.

FACT 29 The Union Jack combines the flags of England, Scotland and the patron saint of Ireland.

FACT 30 The Union Jack first came into use in 1801.

FACT 31 The Union Jack appears on the flags of other countries that were once ruled by British kings and queens.

FACT 32 The flag of England is the cross of St George.

FACT 33 According to legend, the dragon on the flag of Wales is a symbol of the Britons, who fought against invaders 1,500 years ago.

FACT 34 This flag is the Royal Standard of the United Kingdom. It is the flag used by the country's king or queen.

FACT 35 In Scotland, the Royal Standard is different. The three lions of England swap places with the red lion of Scotland.

FACT 36 The cross on Scotland's flag is called a saltire. It is the symbol of Scotland's patron saint, St Andrew.

Western Europe

FACT 37 The flag of France is called *Le Tricolore*, which means "three colours".

FACT 38 The colours of the French flag are based on the cockade, a symbol of the French Revolution (1789–99).

FACT 39 The flag of Germany was first used from 1919–33.

FACT 40 From 1945–90, Germany was split into two countries with different flags.

FACT 41 Switzerland is one of only two countries to have a square flag.

FACT 42 The coat of arms on Spain's flag shows symbols of five kingdoms that joined together to form the country.

FACT 43 The orange and green on Ireland's flag represent two warring sides. The white is a symbol of peace.

FACT 44 Legend has it that Denmark's flag miraculously dropped from the sky during a medieval battle.

FACT 45 Denmark's flag has been used since 1625. That makes it the world's oldest national flag.

Copenhagen, Denmark

Eastern Europe

FACT 46 The flag of Russia was first used as the symbol of the Tsars, or Russian Emperors.

FACT 47 From 1917–91, Russia was part of the USSR and had a different flag.

FACT 48 St Basil's Cathedral was built on the orders of Russia's first Emperor, Ivan the Terrible.

St Basil's Cathedral, Moscow

Czech Republic

FACT 49 The flag of the Czech Republic used to be the same as the flag of Poland. The blue triangle was added to make it different.

Poland

FACT 50 The dark red colour on the flag of Latvia is known as "carmine".

FACT 51 The Latvian flag was banned while the country was part of the USSR. It came back into use when the USSR broke apart.

FACT 52 The pattern on the flag of Belarus represents the country's flowers and plants.

FACT 53 The flag of Slovenia shows Mount Triglav, the country's highest peak. It is 2,864 m (9,396 ft) high.

Western Asia

FACT 54 The flag of Israel shows the Star of David, a symbol of the Jewish religion.

FACT 55 The flag was created when Israel was formed in 1948, as a homeland for the Jewish people after World War II.

FACT 56 The flag of Iran includes a holy Islamic phrase repeated 22 times. The phrase runs along the edges of the red and green bands.

FACT 57 The writing on the flag of Saudi Arabia is an Islamic prayer written in Arabic script.

FACT 58 Because the writing on the flag is holy, the Saudi flag is never allowed to touch the ground.

FACT 59 Turkey's flag shows symbols of the Ottoman Empire, which ruled the area for centuries.

FACT 60 The moon and star on Turkey's flag were seen in a dream by the first Ottoman Emperor.

FACT 61 Lebanon's flag shows a cedar tree. Lebanon has been famous for these trees since the time of the Romans, more than 2,000 years ago.

Cedar of Lebanon

19

Eastern Asia

FACT 62 The flag of Nepal is the only national flag that is not a square or rectangle.

FACT 63 The red circle on the flag of Japan represents the rising sun.

FACT 64 By law, the flag of India must be made from a hand-woven cloth called khadi.

FACT 65 The two colours on Pakistan's flag represent different religions living together in peace.

FACT 66 On China's flag, the red colour and five-pointed stars are symbols of the ruling Chinese Communist Party.

FACT 67 The Sri Lankan flag shows a lion holding a sword, representing the bravery of the Sri Lankan people.

FACT 68 The flag of Turkmenistan includes designs used in the country's traditional carpet weaving.

FACT 69 The building on the flag of Cambodia is Angkor Wat, a huge ruined temple.

FACT 70 Yin and Yang, the red and blue shapes on the flag of South Korea, represent balance in the universe.

Northern Africa

Several countries in north-east Africa use symbols of Arabic culture on their flags.

The bird on the flag of Egypt is called the Eagle of Saladin, after a historical leader of Muslim armies.

The green, yellow and red on the flag of Senegal show unity with other African countries.

FACT 74
The flag of Tunisia shows symbols of the Ottoman Empire, which Tunisia was once part of.

FACT 75
The colours of Ethiopia's flag come from the Ethiopian Empire, which lasted more than 800 years.

FACT 76
The yellow star in the centre of the Ethiopian flag signifies the country's bright future.

FACT 77
Niger's flag colours represent dry desert in the north and fertile land in the south.

FACT 78
The desert shown on Niger's flag is the Sahara, the world's largest hot desert. The Sahara spreads across much of Northern Africa.

Sahara Desert

Southern Africa

The flag of South Africa was created in 1994.

The "Y" shape on the South African flag represents two groups – black and white people – coming together in unity.

The flag of Zimbabwe shows a statue found in the country's ancient capital, Great Zimbabwe.

The flag of Swaziland is decorated with a traditional shield and spears.

The colours on the shield represent black and white people living together peacefully.

The bird in the middle of the flag of Uganda is a grey crowned crane.

The flag of Malawi features a rising sun, a symbol of hope for the future.

In 2010, the government of Malawi tried out a new flag. It was so unpopular that they had to bring back the old one.

The flag of Lesotho shows a traditional hat or *mokorotlo*.

Mokorotlo hat

Oceania

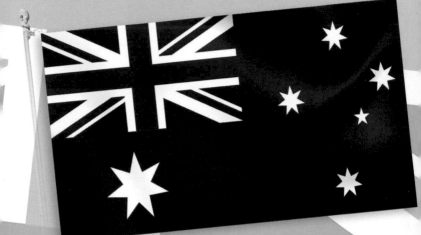

 FACT 88 Australia is part of the Commonwealth (see fact 102). Its flag includes the Union Jack.

FACT 89 Flags in Oceania often show the Southern Cross, a group of stars that can only be seen south of the Equator.

 FACT 90 The flag of Vanuatu shows a gold boar's tusk, a symbol of wealth.

FACT 91 The bright blue of the flag of Fiji represents the Pacific Ocean.

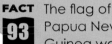

FACT 92 The flag of Fiji features the island's crops: bananas, cocoa, sugar cane and coconuts.

FACT 93 The flag of Papua New Guinea was designed in a competition. The winner was a 15 year old girl called Susan Karike.

FACT 94 The three waves on the flag of Kiribati stand for the three groups of islands that make up the country.

FACT 95 The frigate bird on the flag of Kiribati is a common seabird in the South Pacific Ocean.

Global
Organisations

As well as countries, many
organisations have their own
flags which can be seen
around the world.

The flag of the United Nations shows all the
world's countries working together peacefully.

Symbols of peace are important to the
United Nations because it was created after
World War II to prevent such a conflict from
happening again.

The European
Union is a
group of
countries that work
together to improve
trade. Its flag has
12 stars representing
the people of Europe.

FACT 100 The Arab League was founded in 1945 to help countries in North Africa and the Middle East work more closely together.

FACT 101 The Red Cross and the Red Crescent work to protect people in danger from starvation, disease and war.

FACT 102 The Commonwealth of Nations is a group of countries that were once part of the British Empire.

FACT 103 If you were to group the countries of the Commonwealth together, they would cover about 20 per cent of the world's land.

FACT 104 The flag of the Antarctic Treaty represents an agreement to keep Antarctica open for scientific research.

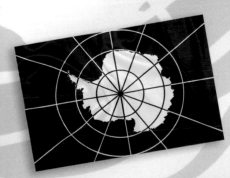